The 36
From Ripon

Caroline Matusiak

Q

First Published in Great Britain in 2024

7 Grape Lane, Petergate, York YO1 7HU
Tel: +44 (0)1904 635967
Email: info@quacks.info
Website: radiusonline.info

Quacks Books is an imprint of Radius Publishing Ltd

A CIP catalogue record for this book is available from the British Library.

ISBN: 978-1-912728-84-8

Set on a page size of 148 x 210mm printed by offset lithography on an one hundred gsm chosen for its sustainability.

For
Ava and Sofi

Contents

Ripon Jewel

Sun gold sheet backs the evening horn blow
casting golden strip to set and to trace
with dull amber stone and garnet shadow
Saxon gates radiating market place.
Ripon, a jewel, laid on a casket
finely inset with rivers Ure and Skell,
Kirkgate where Turner stopped to sketch
painting Hackfall Wood and Mowbray Castle.

Priceless gem of Ripon cultured for all
fine folk fiestas of creative arts
street theatre, dance, music recital
opera and poetry in the park.
This beauty we can all appreciate
in it, find a voice and participate.

 white horse

(*Sutton Bank*)

the galloping cloud horse
bucks and rears
amid the unfettered field of sky
sparking wild silver sunlit shoes
snorting wet jowled
its breath twisting mist
into the iron shod cloud
winds rolling and ripping
fine sweat glistens
a steer let loose in a wild place

a bird flies from horizon tree
over the pallid infinite
patched vale of york

glancing down at the chalk chip
crumble of white horse
cut like a cookie
from grass bank
moss and hair tuft
greening its flank
its legs stopped in
a century of time
limestoned loin
old greying mare
its progeny
the shapeshifter cloud
that trots the skies
mirroring the vision that
dropped this foal in chalk
on a bare bank

and the elysian fields
above that fill its dream
blindly nosing the bare back wind
hope gliding on a thermal
an unbridled dream
of cantering meadow
and lush unbroken will

 Awe - some

Somehow
when I step in this door
Something
is left behind.
Life's litter blows away across the grass.

Somewhere
in a momentary eclipse
an aqua realm of water opens
lifting me, to and fro, in the surge of
words that paint
paint that rhymes
stitches that cross and knot.
I am adrift on a swirling eddy
of infinite possibilities
that reach to take my hand
or elude a finger touch
as they slide into horizon blue.

Somewhat
enraptured, I deep dive
into this entrancing water world
where pen and brush
snorkel their way down
to rocks that give up their sound
and fronded weeds their hidden lives
words shell, paint shingles
stitches unpick their patterning
until, needing to breathe,
I call the dive,
ascending, feet flicking, above.

Someplace
where the garden fork leans against a garage wall
where spiders spin on dusty boxes
and there's a very cold cup of tea
that's been waiting for
Sometime

 Green Man

Five o'clock shadow of
purpled floating bluebells
vein the face of the wood.
Eyebrows arch quizzical in
the tree tunnel of jointed twig.
The bud-leaf hairline of branches
startle the sky.
Rugged jowl of grey trunk
leans to inhale a
starlit wild garlic infusion
of musk seduction
amongst the white beaded necklets
of straggled nettle strings.
The hurdling brook chuckles
through stone chattering teeth.
Blossoms spare kisses
pale the forest floor
gently
on memories, mossy but green.
A twig snaps.
The see-saw call of birdsong
sharpens
and on the path
a deer track
where he has been.

 owl hunting

I woke to
owl hunting

circlets of soprano
looping beneath the planets
in silver liquid ring
the field freezing
with sugar ice
and scuttles of fear

white feather shuttlecock
slicing the night trees
rustlings
white blank heart face
with bead shine eye
turns, calls, spells
a shrill silence
in a glance
and a wave of wing

I slept to
owl haunting
that faraway forest of dream

a l i l y l u l l a b y

to float adrift a while in a pool   of watchful
water lilies   waxen   white florets   folding
   origami circles   of golden orange   hairpin crowns
            when tiptoes
            no longer
          touch the
        floor of the lake
      gravelled with time
     mosaic diary
 of the undone
  and done to
     then to
     s u s p e n d
      in water
  foot paddling
   in reflecting
   marbling sky
     resting as
        leaves skim by
          let the
            c o o l
             of the water
              heal
           heat of the day
         take the
         tumult in   string
   ripples a w a y   swavering
     there in the water's   long
           fish eye lens   are the

14

stems
     of waterlilies
         caging
        directing unseen
     but now look look   there are the roots
    there is only to swim in between

 fox

there he was
outside the window
in the early morning
hunkered in a hollow
hunting
a sweat of rusted spice
in the dew lush meadow
caught in dawn's blush
inquisitive
inquisitor
alpha provider
sensing
an invader
saw me
without turning

ears sidelong sharp
fine tail singed
with red flush
of fine pelt
low slung
silent authority
of masterful instinct
padding lightly
on felted paws
to dip away
into woodland shades
without turning

The reluctant sash window
finally yields and opens
to the singing wood
at the end of the garden.

I want to fill this room
with the chattering trees'
feathery songs,
with melting menthol air
crisp with scented pine,
to invite in
sierra fringe
sun seeking flower faces
and the raw ginger tang of fox

to fill here
to fill now
to fill me
to my toes end
without ever turning

'that'll be the old hill'

and it was
this ancient neolithic howe
in a sleep of centuries
thistles bearding its dozing face
smiling skywards
at those birds still
darting on electric wing
at those clouds
wiping with linen cloth
the tousled brow of this mound
at that wind
ruffling the unkempt hair
of fringe bobbing grasses

the mystery of ages
lies here, within,
the wisdom of the ancients
resides here
to know that we don't know
to wonder at the mystery

of this back broken cavern
flint sharp bone smoothed
carpeted in rock roof turf
a way marker on the road
and on the sundial of time

warrior tribute
tribal statement
water worship

at this way marker we stand
for even now we build
cult of celebrity
wall of warning
ceremonial gate
where the sundial shows shadow

this ragged hill
still seduces
still cautions
wired into pub folk talk
of happenings
and dark night dread

this old hill
stone-ager
ever the influencer
on a thread, sacred,
a golden filament
streaming live from
the dawn of who we are

 d a r n i n g

If life were a pullover
It would need darning
after petty beetle nibbles
from jealous back biting
from wear and tear
of tedious elbowing
to find a way
to find a place

If life were a pullover
It would need repairing
the heavy seam splitting
of work weary friction
dragging a humdrum load
unpicking woolly days
on repeat
on repeat

If life were a pullover
It would be unravelling
cuffs fraying with loving
caring and hurting too
too much

If we were a pullover
We would need darning
stitches of rough wool
binding us together
the sequence of pattern
suddenly lost
in threads interweaving
our own creative patch

 Blanketed

Welcome to you
With this coverlet of cosiness

A cuddle in crochet
A weave that warms

A chain mail in links
That clasp and protect

A pilgrimage in shells
To signpost your steps

A coat of merry colours
Rainbow words in wool

A banner of prayer over dipping days
Cashmere cords to lullaby deep night away

Crocheted in clumsiness
Stitches slipping
Fingers treble
Too many or too few
Handmade
Threading silky lustre
As a blessing to you

 Conker fall

I was there

When brown eyes
winked and enticed between clasp of finger leaves
ochre, red-veined, autumn-tired,
offering fruits in prickly baskets.

Children circle
calling, rounding hunters
raising grey sticks in attack
ready for ritual
entangled strings
face to face dance.

The prized still glint above.
Covid spiked. Defiant.

Dodging falling conkers, I pick one up
open the harsh case
loosening it from light sponge bed rest,
hurrying to see
saturnine rings, in nut gloss
hold that soothing silk.

An earthy new planet
for today
just today
tomorrow dulls and hardens.

A time capsule
rooted in a past
I only hear about
growing to a future
I will never know.

My veined fingers
pen this conker in spike letter cases
cushion it on fibrous paper white.
Now it will always gleam
from afar.

Open the page. Out will fall
the shouts, the sunshine
and rolling to my feet still newly-glazed
freshly fallen
that day.

and I am there

 Oceanic

I see an ocean
inside your head
where once we walked
on land

the tide has drifted
slowly slowly in
leaving me
behind

the current swirls
around your feet
and calls you
out of reach

I stretch out my hand
but you do not
recognise
the beach

I want to wake you
from this dreamy sleep
but you cannot
be found

I looked to sing
a sunny souvenir
but find that it
lies drowned

memories from ocean floor
are floating up to you
you grasp them

with a child's delight
and hold them close
once more

I throw a line from yesterday
but you don't know
what to do
it slips your hands
and leaves your mind
struggling and askew

you're drifting drifting
out to sea delighting
in its touch, chatting to the fishes
and to the clouds above

I cannot see you now
for tears that roll in
with this tide

I just want to take your arm, my dear,
and see you know my face
but you are smiling out at sea
the sea kelp ropes around my thigh
and I am left alone, right here,
on this stony place

 Lectio Divina

Meditation in Melrose Abbey

This stone baked warm mellow
of saintly sandstone block
gives out its hidden holiness.
God's breath scripted in red tracery.
The falling arches ornate flourish
capture the brokenness of heaven on earth
against the sky's ethereal vellum.

Life's disjointed disappointment
carved in the rollicking features
of chortling gargoyles
mocking our best intents
laying low wistful purity
and life's lived excesses
with ungainly jest solidified
with hammered smirk
eyeing us blindly.

There in the sharp calligraphy
of the low ruins of walls
are the verticals and flicks
spelling a beauty of order
a rose gold carpet page
inscribing a portal to praise.

Sun haloes its resurrected light
through the cursives of a rose window
over all
over time
bread shared on a bench
friendship drunk from a tin cup

fragrance with crushed rosemary
the foot slipping ways
on the busy tessellated tiles
of interlocking days.

For a moment
the mason's chisel
stops
unheard silence
unseen light
exquisite *Incipit*
to the simplicity of God.

Caedmon

Top of the steps stands Hilda's abbey wall
Framed by sea and clover leaf trinity
Skeining wild geese interlace and call
Weaving peace in Celtic eternity
On a light-kissed breeze of Gothic Whitby
Whisper lullaby bells soft lingering
Caedmon opens his arms to the dazzling sky
And feather flutter of angelic wing
This lowly herdsman in a holy dream
Praises Maker in poetry and song
A wellspring of words and music that stream
As he crafts a chalice to hold it in
As it spills from the rim in golden rhyme
To settle the heart's longing for divine

thornborough henges

deferent couples process down the path
seal the sacred moment in a selfie
their sacrifice on a lead sniffing grass
tread the download beat of ceremony
mists rising from the sun cast of grey skin
exhale names and voices on beaded moss
of gathering place; stories singing from stones
of exchange, dispute, a tattoo or loss
only the skylark dips in solemn dances
to court a lover and set the skies trilling
in woven night to find a star string bounces
back from shining earth to heaven spinning
as orion's belt smiles among the stars
beaming hello from ancestors of ours

 Second Spring

What are these?
Pallid paper clusters
of cowslip umbrella
reaching for light's lamp
beneath the fragrant vigour
of lavender street
where tourist bees
lurch full summer
drunk on honey shots

While cowslips wasted
waver unsteadily
on anorexic stem
graveyard shift
overtime overtired
their listing yellow moons
waxing mellow in hot noon
waning in fatigue
of unnatural dream

Hanging on for duvet day
in deep earth's dark blanket

Thirsting for takeaway top up
in coffee grain loam
watery petal lemon
eyes closing against
this garish sunny mirror
shine of unending summer
sun blinded, thread thin,
a nervous breakdown
in green burn out

Shaken from sleep
biorhythm busted
earth erupting
its deathly sleepers

Is this the second coming?
Of spring?

 Luskentyre

Bay at the edge of the ocean
Permed wave fringe curling sandwards
White whisker crested from Arctic tundra
Unyielding sea languorously pleated
With ice glint of Viking eye
Bejewelled in dull turquoise
A dusk cloak set with steel grey brooch
Rocks pin fathoms in stillness
Seabirds slapped and torn across a helmet sky
Crying in Jurassic plaintiff
Against the keeling certainty of unchanging centuries

 In Columba's footsteps

There is serpentine in the soul
but I could not find it.
I strode the beach
I turned the stones
I search the life known
but still I cannot find it.

There is something here
quite smooth, quite green
quite hard and dull to see
but it is not the stone I seek
only a marble imitation.

I bathe my feet
in the fresh cooling cleansing
of Columba's frothing sea waves
where stones cut in my sole.
I can hardly walk in jagged pain.
This grit follows in my boot
it chips, it stings as I walk
like stone in an oyster shell.
Turning out my boot
there lies the lucid greening
of translucent light
serpentining my stone-edge life.
I find it was there all the time.

 wintering

stubbled
snow flecked
with winter age

liquid eyes
grazing
give back
the brown tarn
where the
cotton grass
waves
even now

together

we walk
rucksacked
weathering
storms

stand

with our shoulders
to the howling heave
as life tears
at all we are

inviting
in life
and each other
swaying
in breezes
like birches

silver perpendicular
paper rolled
leaves littering
gustily windwards

it is in this
meandering
along pathways
opening
that our
lives embrace
reaching
for comfort
for sharing
for laughter

we look up
at tops climbed
and around
at landscapes
of peace and pain
clambered
and down
at mingled footprints
on a puddled path

nosterfield

follow the blue splinter dragonfly home
to this estuarine wet grassmap scrape
    where striding distant birds black-angle stick bone
      footprint notation across flat silt drape
       their music flute falls and piping treble
   butterflies in brown skirts flirt and scatter
  where roman adjusted leather sandal
   on a way known by hunter gatherer
    and the quarry grinds and raises gravel
     along the spit   from hawk   birds merge and swoop
      wader beaks now shingle shift and shovel
       while little egret state plumes bow on loop
   osprey skylined   waiting   eye stripes swivel
        tree top commander new age sentinel

Ripon Cathedral

so treading lightly, now quiet, now calm,
listening to brown birds singing plainsong
looking to catch a blue sky cloud of balm
as tonsured sparrows murmur along
inside the nave, angelic arches stoop
to catch the sighs as faint footsteps falter
vigils for health, for rest, prayer or soup
look east for hope rising at the altar
other times intoning other voices
Owen writing of war and its pity
we all face that melody of choices
St Wilfrid chanted a church and city
back in life's cacophonous whirl I see
there's the stillness of the crypt within me

 # Whitbarrow

Ebony raven craw craws
from under jagged scar
Its clairvoyant eye
revealing an intruder
halting on clint and grike
of this harsh erratic pavement
A day scented with juniper that
crouches back bent wind torn

Traveller climbs through net
of dumbing mist face hooded
Hoping for a change of weather
Hoping for change

The mystic raven lifts its carrion claw
Its dark beak beckoning
bearing ancient wisdom
of folklore fable

Walking in a dream of mist
Here is raven
Blue black feather wing
ready to lift
ready to fly
signalling that move
from dull earth gravity
to light ethereal sky

An invite from tales twice told
to seek the hidden
so easily over trodden
To look between the naked slabs
to find a world of

fern finery, urchin rock roses
rare red helleborine

Covered like a view
behind grey mist
As a curtain corner lifts
there are the hills
pencilled in pink purple
woodland etched
in lime leaf shade
sky wash of patient blue

Only wait
until the mist opens its arms
to inner journeying

 Spring Wood

I know a path
To an Ancient Wood
Of pale green enchantment
Where tiny leaf buds pepper
Crooked grey stalks
Angular and enduring
Against unyielding blue

My path steps
Through unkempt meadow
Busy with lapis insects
Cushioned with dandelion suns
And yellow celandine
Spilling in star bright confusion.
Buttery brimstone lazily flap.

The skylark's upward
Trembling trill shrills
In warning.
A tractor growling consumes its bed.
Bird calls quivering
Against the groan of diesel.

 Clouded over

Yes, Yes, there is a cloud,
And we are in it,
You and I
Swaddled in this tomb of white
Sepulchred together
Not seeing eye to eye
Love's language lost
In chipped words of white granite
Our heat dampening to grey drizzle
Desire muffled in a cotton cocoon.

Cloudscape paths form, and fade
Into a wall of gloss glaze
Where sorry stings and needles
Freezing in glass splinters.
Yes, in this cloud
The frost deeply bites,
With stalactite incisor,
Sharply ices
Each warm, falling, hurting, tear.

Darkening skies

Time to take a night walk
beneath dark sky
no longer face down
pavement passing
clicking under the heels
rolling work diary
pages turning in a similar
familiar way

Time to look up
life was born
life has died
black gnarled sinew trunk
has bud and blossom
its paper white petals
flaking on snow
like stars in a day sky

Time to stroll
down country lane
beck of rain rising
gurgling along grey drain
catching the silk
of milky moonlight
whitening the rib
tree bones

Time to welcome
embrace of darkness
soft warm
of its covering rest
there with pale citrus

day fading
find a thrill
of stars burn there
eternally pulsing
secrets in silver

 Canyoning

Let go!
As life takes you
along its watery path.
Fall from your sky, air brushing skin
pinch the nose, hold the breath
wait for that surface slap
awaken every sense, bubble every nerve

Go down, down
below your depth
in other world quiet
as water folds above
baptismal cleansing, new life rapture
go go go
free flow the gorge
slip sleeking like a grey seal
slither gritted pitted limestone
uneven boulders below
rush that flow, flow in that rush
coarse rocks
bump, bite and scuff sore
searing the mind's cavern

Stepping out on stone bank
heart wounds glisten, sheen like water
wear them as dripping satin
in a shy beauty
covering
the day, the hurting

 # Overheard

(at Ripon Wetlands)

Waiting   watching
still the surprise
whirr whirr of wings
in synchronising swirl
a glinting lift
in the bird newsprint sky
against the palest pink eve
the lurching turn
of beat flap wings
the joy of unison
the dull dapper
city suited starlings
pin striping the lilac sky
the evening commute
rush hour for the roost
roundabouting
then stretching
along a one way street
the murmuration
dips and dives
over skeletal tree line
nature's compelling compass
magnetizes
mesmerises

Boots mud stamped
Toes wet frozen
Ice finger gloves
but inside a coat
racing in relief
to an unseen heartbeat
the flitter of soft wing rising

 Winterbourne

It is that time
when that surge
of spiking loss
tears its tears
spearing upwards
from a lingering
dormant stream bed
quietly quietly
from behind closed lids

This grieving season
of orange ochre
when berried haws
reveal their thorns
in painful paper cuts
and heavy rooted contemplation
of what was
and the stifled bud
of what could have been

And I, I am wrapped in a shroud
of sharp lily scent
that stings in stuffiness
bound in coarse linen
of memories churning
in the slipstream of bereft
carrying me along
its gripping undercurrent
it will not let me go
until I have lived
relived and only then
relieved, will it let go

As grief streams
I lay back and float
among its whispering grasses
like Ophelia singing
among the fragrance of thyme
like Ophelia staring at
that sunless sky
stridently blazing
with emptiness in
white vapour wisps

This underground grief
rises, cradling me
in its watery casket
cooling as pain burns
rocking along in sobs
to a clear pool
where I make a grab
at overhanging hope
hidden among leafy days
where I stand
foot paddling
in refreshing waters
and rinse the face of memory
and pick up those
clothes of daily life
left scattered in haste
along its grassy bank
ready to step the stones
to find a path
through the green nettles'
stinging grasp

 Until

Waiting
wraps itself like a wraith
around time
a dampening shroud
a white out of now
into a checkout queue
of blank looks
and misted stares

Waiting
that nether world
where what we want to do
and where we are
stand mirror still
on a platform of cancelled trains

Waiting
time frozen
in a hoarfrost Havisham veil

Trapped
an insect spectre
suspended from
spider web dullness
to be on hold
waiting
just waiting
until

Or waiting
an expectant time
when pregnant hope waits
purposefully

as distant stars
of plans and dreams
nurture a growth
into quiet
anticipation

Time to reflect
the wonder of waiting
to ponder
to prepare a cradle
for possibilities
as until becomes when

 Green Lane

Wearily dragging muddy hem
the linear lane threads
within gritted skirting of drystone dyke
embroidered with moss
indented by toothy fern
moss cross stitch starlets
pad the sheltering trod
of splattered clogs

Snowdrop hood hangs heavy
to hold out driving rain
memories mushroom
from beneath brown leaves
drenched and hopeless

Between here and there
between now and then
the lane winds
celtic smudges
of white linen lichen
paint slow history
on grey silurian slate

A tree erupts from stone
its thinning birch twigs
an overhanging shawl
of black lace grieving

This weight of wall
pierced by root life
that will be heard
that will be known

Whispering its woes
of hard living and stiff joints
lane puddled with empty plates
filled with freshening rain scent
of the trodden and forgotten

The burden across the back
too heavy to carry
too tightly strapped
to lay down

Snow drop weeps
downy fern drips
powder catkins hang trembling

At last
slithers of green spring
start to filter felted path

 Negative Space

I
It is the spaces between us
that count
They tell the story
They catch the breath
They outline the edge of life

And in that space
A hand waved air
A table trembled
A seat fell back
And a coffee cup rolled over the floor

II
The story is in the sky
lining this little piece
of heaven's hill. Blue, grey
turquoise wash the air
with tranquility - the
negative space - the silence
a respite from the ardour
a backrest to float the load
to lean into its cushion
The white light bright
it blinds, it streaks - be dazzled
and later climb the hill
knowing that feet won't touch
the ground

III
The spaces around us
make way - as life
is peopled in shadow
heads turn
mouths open
words v i b r a t e
laughter escapes
this flowing negative space
it silhouettes our features
draws rings around us
makes way for what we do
but is stranger to who we are

IV
It is the spaces between us
that know
In the pheromones that signal
alarm and attraction
In the negative space
we communicate
without ever saying a word

V
Moving towards each other
the space between recedes
drawing back, billowing, billowing away

negative space surrounds us

We are inside it
in our very own
very positive space

# Sphagnum

A dried weft of sphagnum
slipped from its sleep
between my boot tread,
dormant but alive

Thread cells empty but waiting
to drink thirstily, absorb hungrily,
again and twenty times again, rain water,
rehydrating and reviving

Dry sphagnum plait for battle wounds
a sterile poultice of gauze moss
soaking up pus, blood, pain,
healing without favour

Tramping the rivulets of sticky paths
I see the stooping shadows of worn sisters
mothers, wives, with sacks dripping hope,
moss gathering

Then stamping out the tearful moss
hanging their love out to dry
by the coal blackened range,
hearts knotted

They found the soldier buried overseas
under coarse jacket on lethal wound
a rough swab of bloodied sphagnum,
healing in death

The bog moss pall of peat cradles
the torqued reverence of ancient violence
soldiers culled from uncounted battles,
timeless preserver

As I walk the stone wall dales
the bosom of sphagnum calls to rest
in its foot sinking oblivion
the clanging heads of war power
knowing that its starry cushions
hold no repose for aching lonely loss
that withers those left behind

 Coorie in

Coorie in my dear one
With me beside my shawl
The storm outside is live
It's shrieking like a ghoul

Coorie in my own heart
The fire is building up
Blue lightning snatches
Like fingers at tree top

My knitting needles click
As we watch the fire glow
Logs shuffle in the grate
Soup is boiling on the stove

Outside trees are snapping
Orange shadow covers moon
Webbing all the bushes
Gates creak as if it's doom

Coorie in my dearest
I see fire in your eyes
So warm me in your love
Sit here with me, close by

Coorie in my dear one
Coorie in to me

 Cross
            Country

Snow ice firs lace the sky's bloom
Skis shuffle
                shuffle
                     and
                          slide
to hidden rhythmic beat.
Sky threatens aurora rose
palest green
 bars shooting
   and striking
     in viking
      fury the
       top trees.
   Snow flops.
Falling into the silent waiting.

As I shuffle
            shuffle
Lamplight crystallises snow cake layers.
Sequinned and shimmering
Snow shakes shift from firs.
Shuffle
      shuffle towards the rising smoke of home.

 Wild bilberry ways

Stepping out
to tread the path
silvered by razored
birch bark trunks
throwing breezy leafy
limbs in crowd waves
across a cloud stadium
blue melt sky
mottled leaves
shiver and shimmer
in rainstick sighs

It is time
for that known path
anticipation
tingles the tongue
powers the boots
and sets the taste compass
to 'can't wait'

Here leads the way
wrapped by moor and mountain
with lemon lichen lace
over solemn troll stone faces
gulping fresh sting of air
facing an exhilarating wind
of change and challenge

It is time
rusty autumn sprawls and spreads
her burning shawl
there bilberry bushes,
swaggering greenleaf

dog-toothed kilted celts
braceletted in rouge
pierced with tattoo blue rings
dusky primal runes

'Join us, we are here
the tart sweet sip
will stain face and finger
we are *terroir*
sour by soil dusty with wind
purple rain fill cup'

A season sensation
in its time
on our path
today

Bus to Ripon

On bus 36 sit down, pen steady
Now pass village lanes, the field that floods,
Look, Ripley Cross is coming up already
Then garden centre and busy pubs.
On board there's always some conversation
Of pets or home until someone leaves
With people heading to work or station
I sew and say,'Would you like one of these?'
And then I pack my bag with crochet hook,
At the market place with trumpet loud,
With writing pad and unread book
And step off right in the bustling crowd
But this is not a shopping trip today,
Inside my bag are words in ricochet.

Previously Published

Awesome
New Contexts 5, edited by Ian Gouge Coverstory books 2023

Blanketed
Celebrate! Poems from The Fifth Ripon Poetry Festival 2022, edited by
Andy Croft, Claire Thompson and Sheila Whitfield 2022

Green Man
Creative Juices, Poems from The Sixth Ripon Poetry Festival 2023,
edited by Andy Croft, Katie Scott and Simon Strickland 2023

nosterfield
Creative Juices, Poems from The Sixth Ripon Poetry Festival 2023,
edited by Andy Croft, Katie Scott and Simon Strickland 2023
a winner from this festival

Spring Wood
Celebrate! Poems from the Fifth Ripon Poetry Festival 2022, edited by
Andy Croft, Claire Thompson and Sheila Whitfield 2022